D1085444

Writing:
Stories, Poetry, Song, & Rap

ART TODAY!

Acting: Stage & Screen

Art Festivals & Galleries:
The Art of Selling Art

Comedy & Comedians

Filmmaking & Documentaries

Music & Musicians

Painting

Performing Arts

Photography

Sculpting

Writing: Stories, Poetry, Song, & Rap

ART TODAY!

Writing:
Stories, Poetry,
Song, & Rap

Sara James

Mason Crest

ST. JOHN THE BAPTIST PARISH LIBRARY
2920 NEW HIGHWAY 51
LAPLACE, LOUISIANA 70068

Mason Crest
450 Parkway Drive, Suite D
Broomall, PA 19008
www.masoncrest.com

Copyright © 2015 by Mason Crest, an imprint of National Highlights, Inc. All rights reserved. No part of this publication may be reproduced or transmitted in any form or by any means, electronic or mechanical, including photocopying, recording, taping, or any information storage and retrieval system, without permission from the publisher.

Printed and bound in the United States of America.

First printing
9 8 7 6 5 4 3 2 1

Series ISBN: 978-1-4222-3167-8
ISBN: 978-1-4222-3177-7
ebook ISBN: 978-1-4222-8714-9

Cataloging-in-Publication Data on file with the Library of Congress.

Contents

KEY ICONS TO LOOK FOR:

Text-Dependent Questions: These questions send the reader back to the text for more careful attention to the evidence presented there.

Words to Understand: These words with their easy-to-understand definitions will increase the reader's understanding of the text, while building vocabulary skills.

Series Glossary of Key Terms: This back-of-the book glossary contains terminology used throughout this series. Words found here increase the reader's ability to read and comprehend higher-level books and articles in this field.

Research Projects: Readers are pointed toward areas of further inquiry connected to each chapter. Suggestions are provided for projects that encourage deeper research and analysis.

Sidebars: This boxed material within the main text allows readers to build knowledge, gain insights, explore possibilities, and broaden their perspectives by weaving together additional information to provide realistic and holistic perspectives.

Words to Understand

traditional: The way things have normally been done, often for a long time.

folk music: Music that is passed down from generation to generation. Often the original author is unknown, and it is played on acoustic instruments.

pop: Popular or mainstream music. What "pop" is has changed over the years.

celebratory: Done for a special event or occasion.

publishers: Companies whose job it is to distribute and sell art, including writing.

rejected: Dismissed as being not good enough to publish.

captivated: Had your attention held by something you found very interesting or charming.

civil rights activist: Someone who fights for all humans to have the same rights.

traumatized: Hurt physically or emotionally in a way that lasts a long time.

memoir: A book or story written about your own life.

signed: Signed a contract with a publisher or record label, to give them the right to sell and make money from a work of art.

inducted: Formally let someone into an organization.

revise: Edit, rewrite, or change or improve in some way.

professionals: People who do something for a living, and are often very good at it.

Chapter One

The Purpose
of Writing

Writing has many uses in today's world. In a single day, odds are good you write many, many times. You may write a note to your mom or dad to remind them you need a ride after a music rehearsal or sports practice you have later in the day. You might write down data collected from an experiment in science class, entries in your phone or planner about homework assignments, and an essay for English class. You might text your friends about how you're feeling about your day, whether frustrated, excited, or disappointed. Some of these writing activities might be done electronically on a phone or computer, while others are handwritten with pen and paper—but they all involve words.

The different writing you do during the day also has varied uses. Your note to your mom or dad communicated a task you wanted done, while your data collection was meant for record keeping and scientific discovery. Your texts to your friends express your emotions.

Writing can be yet another thing too—art. Writing that is meant to convey deep ideas and meanings can be considered art. Writing makes people think, just like painting, photography, dance, and other art forms.

Not all writing is art. Instruction manuals and grocery lists aren't art because they just convey information. An instruction manual isn't supposed to make you think about your life in a new way; it's just meant to help you set up a new desk. Your texts aren't poetry—they're just quick expressions of your feelings. These are all ways that writing is useful, though.

TYPES OF ARTISTIC WRITING

Other kinds of writing you've probably already encountered are art, though. Defining which writing is art and which is not can be tricky. It can change depending on who is doing the defining. Most people agree, however, that novels are art. Novels involve storytelling and an artful use of language. They are fictional stories, usually with characters and a full plotline. Their words are chosen carefully, to fit together pleasingly, in a way that inspires emotion in some way, even if that emotion is just entertainment.

Some people only consider literature art. Literature is fictional or nonfictional writing that involves even more creativity. It's meant to serve a higher purpose than just entertainment. We tend to think of literature as high-quality writing that has something important to say about the world, which can limit the definition of art only to books that certain people find particularly good.

Poetry is a type of writing in which language is arranged in ways that people think are meaningful and pleasing. The words poets use are chosen carefully and then put together in a way that is beautiful, meaningful, or thought provoking. Poets have a lot of tools they can use to write poetry. They can make their poems rhyme, or use repetition to drill home a point. They can use alliteration, in which each of their lines or many of the words they use all start with the same sound. Poetry has some things in common with music, in that the sound plays an important role in the meaning and emotional power of the creative work.

A NONSENSE POEM

A good example of the musicality of poetry is Lewis Carroll's "The Jabberwocky." Carroll's work is a nonsense poem—one in which the words themselves don't quite make sense, but the arrangement of the words suggests a meaning that at least is very pretty to hear. Here are the first few lines:

> 'Twas brillig, and the slithy toves
> Did gyre and gimble in the wabe:
> All mimsy were the borogoves,
> And the mome raths outgrabe.

In this one stanza of his poem, Carroll has used two poetic techniques: rhyming ("toves" rhymes with "borogoves") and alliteration ("gyre" and "gimble").

Poet Lewis Carroll.

Prose is basically writing that is not poetry. Prose is the sort of writing you're used to reading in novels or textbooks. It almost always follows **traditional** grammar rules, and it's mostly the words that convey meaning, rather than the structure of the writing. Poetry is written down in lines, sometimes with spaces between them, while prose runs on in large sections that are broken into paragraphs and larger sections such as chapters.

WRITING SPECIALTIES

Some writers do it all, but most have a specialty or two. They focus on a certain type of writing, and get really good at it. Artistic writers include novelists, poets, short-story writers, songwriters, playwrights, and screenwriters.

MUSICAL WRITING AS ART

Most people consider music to be an art, but what about the lyrics—the words that go along with the music? Musical lyrics are art too, especially when they make us think about important topics like love, anger, social issues, and loss.

Different genres of music focus on different topics. In some cases, lyrics are basically poems set to music. Lyrics can be stories, which is common in **folk music**. They can be thoughts and statements about love and letting go of love, like in a lot of **pop** music. They can be ways to transmit religious ideas, as in hymns and gospel music.

Rap lyrics and hip-hop music can be thought of art too, since they're used for more than just sharing information. Rap lyrics are often full of anger about the injustices and harsh realities of urban life, especially for blacks. At other times, though, rap is more **celebratory** and positive. Some rap is about surviving in the city, some is about becoming successful, and some is about fighting racism.

Here are a few lines from a classic rap song called "The Message" by one of the original rap groups, Grandmaster Flash and the Furious Five:

Don't push me cause I'm close to the edge
I'm trying not to lose my head

In another example, the West Coast rapper Blu raps about what happens after death, and how people can reach heaven. Blu's lyrics are very poetic.

Every man has his own heaven
The difference is the way that he envisions it.

FAMOUS WRITERS

There have been thousands and thousands of writers over the years, from ancient poets to modern novelists and musicians. Each one approaches the art of writing in a slightly different way, with something different to say.

For the past few years, J. K. Rowling has been one of the most famous fiction writers. She is, of course, well known for her seven-book Harry Potter series. J. K. Rowling went from someone who simply loved books and writing to being the author of the best-selling book series in history.

She was born Joanne Rowling in 1965. She grew up in England, attended the University of Exeter, and then moved to Portugal to teach English. In 1990, while riding on a train, she came up with the idea for Harry Potter. At the time, she wasn't planning on writing a book—the idea just came to her. She started writing that same day, and kept writing after she moved to Portugal. She eventually moved to Edinburgh, Scotland, to be near her sister. She was struggling to support herself and her daughter at that point, but she kept writing.

Harry Potter and the Sorcerer's Stone took her five years to finish,

J. K. Rowling's incredibly successful Harry Potter series is one of the best-selling book series in history.

and then she sent it off to several **publishers**. She was actually **rejected** quite a few times before she found a publisher who wanted to take on her book. After the first three Harry Potter books had been released, it was clear that the series was something special. The story of a lonely boy entering into a new world of magic and wizardry **captivated** a lot of people both young and old. People couldn't put the books down, and they were eager for the rest of the series. They were preordering the fourth book before it came out, ready to read it as soon as it was released.

By the seventh book, released in 2007, pretty much everyone was familiar with Harry Potter and J. K. Rowling. The books had been translated into dozens of languages on sale in many countries and had been made into a movie series. It was the most pre-ordered book in history, and also the fastest selling—it sold 11 million copies in its first day alone.

The Harry Potter series especially received a lot of attention because some people thought the books inspired more children to read. More and more kids were turning to computers, video games, and TV and movies, but Rowling's books sparked an interest in reading.

Rowling continues on as an author, even thought she has finished the Harry Potter series. She has written more novels, this time aimed at adults.

Meanwhile, there are also many famous poets. One of the most well-known and influential is Maya Angelou. Angelou is a poet, writer, and *civil rights activist* with a long and colorful career. She was born in St. Louis, Missouri, in 1928 and then raised by her grandmother in Arkansas. She was sexually assaulted when she was young, and then her uncles killed the man who assaulted her. Angelou was *traumatized* by these events, and she stopped speaking for five years. During that time, she completely gave up on words—but eventually all her pent-up words, thoughts, and feelings came out in her art.

Angelou's artistic career actually began with theater and music, not writing. She studied dance and acting in high school and went on to act in off-Broadway plays; she even released an album. She also joined the Harlem Writers Guild, a group of black writers and artists based in New York City. She didn't publish her writing until 1969, when she wrote a *memoir* called *I Know Why the Caged Bird Sings*. She was the first black American woman to have a best-selling nonfiction book in the United States. In 1971, she wrote a book of poetry called *Just Give Me a Cool Drink of Water 'Fore I Die*.

At this point, Angelou has published just about every form of writing there is. She used her writing skills and her experience to further the civil rights movement, and she worked with both Malcolm X and Martin Luther King, Jr. She has also written essays, novels, screenplays, and cookbooks.

Maya Angelou is one of the most famous American writers of all time.

One of Angelou's most famous poems is "On the Pulse of Morning," which she read at President Bill Clinton's first inauguration. It reads, in part:

The Rock cries out today, you may stand on me,
But do not hide your face.

Bob Dylan is different kind of poet, a musical one. Dylan was born Robert Allen Zimmerman in 1941 in Minnesota. He always liked music, and he formed his own bands in high school. When he got to college, he started singing folk songs at local cafés. In fact, he liked music and singing a lot more than college, and eventually, he dropped out of college.

Dylan moved to New York City, where a lot of folk music was happening. He met his folk music idol Woody Guthrie, and played gigs around the city. One of his performances was reviewed by the *New York Times*, which led to him being **signed** with a record label to produce his first album.

After that, his career took off. He was unique because of his rough voice, and because he wrote his own powerful songs. Dylan often wrote new lyrics to old folk tunes, giving them a modern twist. His second album was filled with protest songs, pointing out the things that were wrong with society in the 1960s, like racism, war, and poverty. His lyrics were so moving and famous that politicians even cited them. Later on in his career, he turned more to rock music, but his lyrics stayed as interesting as ever.

Here's an example of some of his lyrics from one of his most famous songs, "Times They Are A-Changin." The lyrics suggest all of the problems that need fixing, and urge people not to ignore them.

. . . you better start swimmin'
Or you'll sink like a stone
For the times they are a-changin'.

Dylan has continued to write and perform music decade after decade. He has influenced many, many other musicians, was **inducted** into the Rock and Roll Hall of Fame, received a Pulitzer Prize, and is a household name around the United States.

Bob Dylan helped to shape songwriting, singing about politics, love, death, war, and more. Here, Bob Dylan sings with singer Joan Baez in 1963.

THE PROCESS

Every writer creates her work of art differently. Some can just sit down and write out a poem, a lyric, or a short story. Others need to plan ahead, organize their thoughts, and take notes before they can start writing. In most cases, writers need to *revise* what they've written before it becomes final.

Research Project

Find another famous writer, other than the ones mentioned in this chapter, and write a short research paper about him or her using information you find online or in the library. You may choose any sort of writer covered in this chapter. Write a paragraph explaining why we consider this person to be an artistic writer. Then write a paragraph or two about the individual's background and writing style. Finally, write a paragraph about why we consider this person's work influential, and what difference it has made in the world.

J. K. Rowling, for example, did a little of everything. As soon as she came up with the idea for Harry Potter, she started writing. She spent a long time writing chapters, but she also did a lot of revision. In addition, she had to plan out her story. As soon as it looked like her idea was going to become a complicated story told over many books, she had to plan out the details and the characters. There's a lot for one author to keep track of in the Harry Potter books!

The writing process generally follows a few steps, though individual writers may do things differently or complete multiple steps at the same time. The full writing process applies in particular to novels or very long pieces of writing.

First is the prewriting, which involves creating the plot, brainstorming and fleshing out characters, and deciding format. The next step is drafting. This is when the writer does the bulk of the writing. Then comes revising. A published piece of writing is rarely the first thing the author created. Instead, he revised and reread, and then revised again. An author should look at content, format, grammar, and spelling. Sometimes

With a large series of books like Harry Potter, an author must be sure to keep track of the many details of the worlds she's created.

Text-Dependent Questions

1. What is one way to define artistic writing? What are some examples of writing that is not artistic?
2. How is poetry different than prose?
3. Why can we consider music lyrics to be artistic writing?
4. Briefly describe J. K. Rowling's writing process, from the initial idea to the end of the Harry Potter series.
5. What does revising a draft involve?

an author will have an editor to help them make changes. For authors who aren't **professionals**, friends and family members can serve as editors, or the author can just look at it again (and again) herself.

Finally, if a writer is serious about other people reading his work, he publishes it. In the past, an author had to have a publishing company accept a book, poem, essay, or other writing in order to publish it. Today, an author can choose to publish the book herself using many online sources. If you're a self-published author, you might have a harder time getting a big audience, but it's a lot easier to publish yourself than wait for someone else's acceptance. Self-publishing has opened up the world of writing to almost everyone—maybe even you!

Words to Understand

innovation: A creative new and better way of doing things.

epic: A long poem, often about the deeds and achievements of heroes.

mythic: Having to do with legends or stories.

Chapter Two

The History of Writing

Writing involves many different elements, including the script used, the story told, and the purpose. Once human beings invented writing, they used it for many, many different things. We see writing just about everywhere we look—but it wasn't always that way.

SCRIPTS

Language developed much earlier than writing did, but after a while, people realized that being able to record language would be useful. Writing started developing especially after some groups of people

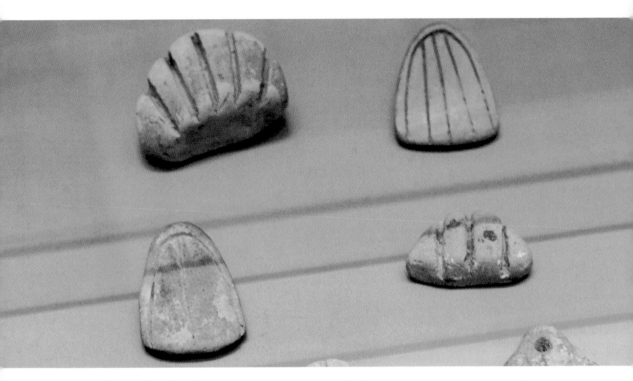

The first kinds of writing were pictures, including lines on accounting tokens.

stopped traveling around to hunt and gather food, and settled down in one place to farm instead.

At that point, many different groups created writing independently of each other. Writing wasn't something invented by one person and then passed down to everyone else. Around the world, lots of humans came up with the idea at about the same time.

As individual people and families owned and farmed land, they wanted a way to keep track of what they owned and what their land produced. These early forms of writing were mostly just pictures. If a farmer wanted to remember that a bag of grain was his, he would put a stamp with a picture on a clay token for record keeping. In ancient

АБВГГДЕЄЖЗ
ИІЇЙКЛМНОПР
СТУФХЦЧШЩ~
ЬЮЯ 1234567890.,
АБВГГДЕЄЖЗИІЇЙ
КЛМНОПРСТУФХЦЧ
ШЩЬЮЯ

The Cyrillic alphabet is quite different from the English alphabet. Languages around the world use different alphabets, from Cyrillic to Arabic.

Syria, a circular token with a cross on it meant "sheep." Other tokens had different patterns of lines to mean different things, including numbers. Writing also made collecting taxes, building cities, and maintaining an army a lot easier.

Later on, scripts became more complicated. They started to represent ideas, not just objects in the world. Different groups of peoples started creating their own scripts, so that not everyone around the world could read the same writing.

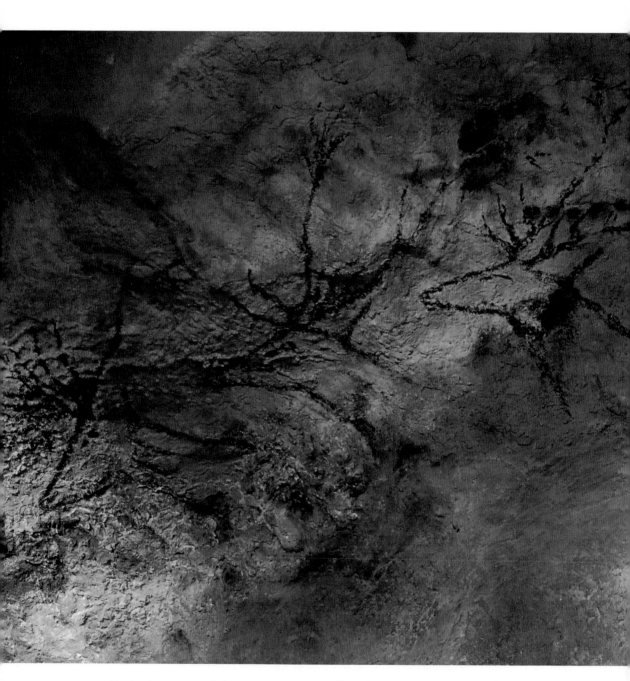

Early drawings of deer on a stone wall in the Lascaux Caves in France.

Make Connections: Paleography

Someone who studies ancient letters and alphabets is called a paleographer. Paleographers study changes in writing over time, and are experts when it comes to dating newly discovered artifacts that contain writing. They can also translate really old writing, using their knowledge of ancient languages and writing systems. Paleographers often work for universities and museums.

The Egyptians developed an early alphabet, where each picture symbol represented a particular sound. For example, one symbol—called a pictograph—meant "water" and was pronounced "nu." Over time, the same pictograph came to represent the sound of "n," rather than just water. Alphabetic writing was much easier to learn. You only had to learn two or three dozen symbols for each sound, rather than the thousands of pictographs that were necessary before. More everyday people could learn how to write, not just people in charge of the government, military, and religion.

During the early history of writing, people used it just to keep accounts of farm and trade goods. After a few thousand years, though, some people started using writing for other reasons. They wrote down the names of the dead so they could be remembered. Kings had their adventures and accomplishments written down. People used writing to teach children. Writing became a lot more like the writing we're used to today.

These days, we still have a lot of different scripts, and all are useful for writing as art. This book is written with the Latin alphabet, but people also use the Arabic alphabet, the Cyrillic (Russian), the Greek (we

Sometimes literature inspires other art forms, and Homer's writing has been giving ideas to artists for hundreds of years. This pottery from the fourth century BCE portrays Homer's hero, Odysseus.

actually get the word "alphabet" from the Greek language), the Hebrew, the Hangul (Korean), and Indic alphabets. Other places, like China and Japan, use language that is more like pictographs.

Today, we're still inventing new ways of writing. Think about emoticons used online and in texts. Emoticons in the form of smiley faces help express emotions that otherwise might not come across in writing. Using symbols for emotions is an *innovation* in writing!

STORYTELLING

While writing itself has a pretty long history, the idea behind writing—telling a story—is even older. For as long as humans have existed, we've been telling stories to each other, even if we couldn't always write them down. In fact, one of the things that distinguishes people from animals is the ability to tell a story.

The earliest proof of storytelling is the Lascaux cave paintings in southern France. The cave paintings show lots of large animals like cattle, horses, and deer, and one human being. Researchers think the paintings tell a simple story about hunting and rituals, though a lot of information has been lost with the years. The Lascaux cave paintings are thought to be about 17,000 years old, but probably people were telling stories to each other even before that.

Sometimes, old stories that had been retold for a long time were eventually written down. A good example is Aesop's fables, stories that had moral points. Aesop was an ancient Greek storyteller who may have lived in the 500s BCE. People are unsure whether Aesop really existed or not, but in any case, the stories attributed to him proved to be popular. They were told and retold for hundreds of years before they were written down. Now Aesop's fables have been translated into most major languages around the world so that everyone can enjoy them.

The first story that was actually written down was the **epic** of Gilgamesh, a **mythic** Mesopotamian king who lived a long time ago. The epic is a long poem that tells the story of Gilgamesh's adventures and journey to find immortality. The oldest version of the epic was written about 4,000 years ago on big stone tablets with an old form of writing called cuneiform. Writers made wedge-shaped marks with reeds on tablets, which paved the way for many more modes of future writing.

Other important and old stories include many religious texts like the Bible, the Qur'an, and the Hindu Vedas. These stories have had an enormous impact on the world. Religious stories explain how the world was created; they set down rules for people's behaviors; and they tell people how to practice their religion. Many cultures that don't have written religious texts also still tell stories about gods and other spiritual forces that shape how that culture works.

Stories of all sorts still play a big part in our lives. We watch stories on TV and in movies. We hear them on the radio or from our friends and family. We read about them in books, newspapers, magazines, and online. Without stories, writing wouldn't be very entertaining or artistic!

Once people combined scripts and stories, we had literature. Writing that documents crop yields or religious taxes might be interesting to historians, but it isn't generally considered literature or art. Writing that tells stories and conveys meanings about ideas and emotions is literature.

Examples of literature exist from all around the world. *The Epic of Gilgamesh* represents one of the earliest forms of literature. Today's literature comes from all corners of the globe. Wherever people write, there are authors.

POETRY

Poetry is a pretty ancient art form. The word poetry comes from the Greek language; it means, "I create." However, poetry was created way before the ancient Greeks, and even before written language.

Some researchers think poems were used by early agricultural societies as a way to convince the gods to give them good harvests. Poetry was also probably used to tell stories and pass down history from generation to generation before writing, as it is still used that way today in some places. Some of these poems were written down later on.

Epic poems are very long, complex poems that tell a story. One of the most famous epic poems is Homer's *Odyssey*, which tells the story of a man returning from war to his home, and his many adventures trying to get there. No one knows for sure when Homer lived, but researchers think it was sometime between the eleventh and seventh centuries BCE.

The *Ramayana* is a Sanskrit epic poem that passes down Hindu

Make Connections: DJ Kool Herc

DJ Kool Herc is known as the godfather of hip-hop. He was born Clive Campbell in Jamaica and moved to the Bronx in the 1960s. He DJed parties, playing a mix of disco, R&B, funk, soul, and more, calling out to the audience to get excited and dance. What made his style especially unique was his focus on the "break," which was the part of the song that featured heavy drumming and was easy to dance to. Kool Herc and his followers created the hip-hop way of life, including the way of dressing, breakdancing, talking, and more.

values and beliefs. Poems such as these could be recited for audiences who couldn't read or write.

Things tend to be easier to remember word for word if they are in poem—or song—form. Maybe you've learned the names of the American states through the song that often taught to young students! Learning all fifty states by heart is much easier when they're set to a poem form. The alphabet song is another good example of using poem form to teach something.

Once writing was invented, authors used it to write down poems. Many poems became shorter. Instead of telling stories, poems were now often about things like love, loss, and sadness.

One of the world's greatest poets was William Shakespeare, who lived in England back in the sixteenth century. He wrote 154 poems called sonnets during his day, which are almost as well known as his plays. Sonnets are fourteen-line poems that have a very specific structure. Many of Shakespeare's plays also include sonnets.

Poets have continued to write and recite poetry around the world. Thousands of poets over the years have composed all sorts of poems.

Graffiti was the visual art form that went along with rap, another part of the hip-hop culture.

Today, modern performance poetry and poetry slams are making oral poetry popular again. Poetry slams are contests in which poets read their own poems aloud, competing for the best poem.

RAP

The history of rap as an art form is pretty new. Rap became a musical genre in the 1970s, although its roots go back before that time. West

Research Project

The history of writing is too long to fit in one book! Pick one of the following styles of artistic writing and research it some more: the novel, the short story, poetry, music lyrics, or rap. For whichever type you choose, research its earliest origins, its progression through history, and how it looks today. Find out the famous writers and famous works of the category you choose. Then use what you've learned and write your own song, poem, rap, or short story about the writing you researched.

African music brought to the United States by slaves during early American history especially influenced rap and hip-hop music. Other influences include jazz, disco, rock, and Jamaican music.

Rap mixes spoken word and poetry with rhythms and beats. It usually rhymes, and often talks about life in the city. Rap is just one part of the whole hip-hop culture, which also includes things like breakdancing, DJing, and graffiti.

Rap started out in the Bronx in New York City. No one person invented it (though several claim they did). Instead, many artists working on their own and together at around the same time created the new genre known as hip-hop. DJ Kool Herc, Afrika Bambaataa, Grandmaster Flash, and Kurtis Blow are all well-known figures from the early rap years. They DJed house parties and parties at other local spots around the Bronx.

Rap didn't stay in the Bronx for long. The first rap group to make a recording was the Sugarhill Gang, who produced "Rapper's Delight" in

DJ Kool Herc helped create the sound of hip-hop.

Text-Dependent Questions

1. What change in human history led to the first written scripts? Why?
2. Why was the invention of alphabetic writing important?
3. What is the earliest evidence people have that even ancient humans were storytellers?
4. How did early people use poetry?
5. Name at least three musical influences on rap.

1979. Young people in urban areas all over the country took it up, and soon the West Coast had a thriving rap scene along with the East Coast.

Now rap has become mainstream pop music, and has spread around the world. American rap has influenced musical artists in Africa, the Caribbean, Europe, Asia, and beyond. Every country it has spread to has changed it a little bit, making rap its own.

Rap is a good example of the way writing can be an art form that changes the world. It's also a good example of how writing as an art form can be part of successful careers that earn individuals thousands, even millions of dollars. It's just one of the many ways that writing can be turned into a business.

Words to Understand

specialized: Having to do with a specific skill or topic.
marketing: Advertising and selling a product.
distributing: Getting a product out to the people who will buy it.
established: Already having succeeded at something.

Chapter One

Chapter Three

The Business of Writing

Writing isn't just an art—it's an artistic business too. Many people want to be able to make a living while doing what they love. Turning writing into a business or career can be tough, but if you're dedicated to making it work, you just may find yourself some success.

Before you enter the business world of writing, though, it helps to understand it. The more you know before you start out, the more likely you are to succeed.

35

Working at home can be great, but it takes hard work to keep to a writing schedule.

Many writers who make their own schedules choose to go to a coffee shop or office space to avoid the distractions of working at home.

WORKING FOR YOURSELF

Most artistic writers work for themselves. They decide what they want to write and how they want to write it. Then they try to get it published by convincing other people that they've written something worthwhile. According to the U.S. Bureau of Labor Statistics, about two-thirds of all writers were self-employed in 2012.

Writers who work from home can choose to work wherever they'd like. They can work at a home office, in a library, at a rented office space, or in a café. They only need access to a pen and paper or a

Many writers find work at newspapers as journalists, editors, copywriters, or bloggers.

Make Connections: Working for Others

A few writers work for other people as employees, though they tend not to be artistic writers. For example, journalists work for newspapers or other news sources, while copywriters work for advertisers and big businesses. The U.S. Bureau of Labor Statistics says that the top industries that employed writers in 2012 were the information industry; professional, scientific, and technical services; the arts, entertainment, and recreation industry; and educational services.

computer. Songwriters who are also musicians may work in a studio space.

Beginning writers usually work part time at writing, especially if they haven't released a work yet. Without sales, a writer hasn't made money yet through her work! A writer might choose to work another job in the same field. For example, he might work for a publishing company, a bookstore, an online magazine, a newspaper, or a library. Or he may also have a job that has nothing to do with writing.

Writers who work for themselves are essentially creating their own business. It might not have a storefront and an official name, but their activities as writers are still businesses.

PUBLISHING

A writer needs to understand the ins and outs of the publishing business if he hopes to get his work professionally published. At some point, a

Kindle
The #1 Bestselling Product on Amazon

Order now: $139 Wi-Fi | $189 Free 3G+Wi-Fi

king At Right Now

E-books and the Internet make self-publishing easier than ever before. Writers can sell their writing themselves, rather than going through a publisher, and reach new fans through websites like Amazon.com.

writer working on a novel, short story, or poems will probably work with a publisher if she hopes to become a professional.

There are different kinds of publishing companies. Most people think of the big publishers, large companies that put out the majority of books read by everyday people. They have been around for a long time, and they have acquired other publishing companies along the way. In fact, very recently there were six big publishers, but now there are only five, because Penguin Books and Random House merged into Penguin Random House.

The big five publishers have name recognition and huge audiences because they know how to market and distribute their books to a lot of people. Each company has several imprints, which are divisions within the company. Each imprint has its own kind of books it publishes, like nonfiction, children's books, or young adult. However, all the imprints in a publishing company still belong to that business. Writers often dream of getting their work published by one of these companies.

However, there are also many small publishers out there. Writers with very **specialized** books may seek out smaller companies that match their topics. For example, Chelsea Green Publishing releases books about sustainable living, including gardening, cooking, and renewable energy. Other small publishers focus on poetry, religion, and more. The publisher who produced this book focuses on educational books!

Self-publishing is also taking off. Today, more books are self-published than are published through a traditional business. When a writer self-publishes, he is in charge of the whole thing—writing, laying out the words into book form, illustrations if necessary, **marketing**, and **distributing**. While self-publishing is more work, it also gives the writer more control over the process. Instead of waiting to hear back from publishers who might make drastic changes to the work, a writer can just publish something he's happy with already, something he thinks will be interesting to other people.

Research Project

Find a website that is dedicated to helping writers self-publish their writing. Explore the website to find out how much it costs, what the writer has to do, and what the end result is (for example, does the website produce e-books, hard copies of books, or both). Does the website seem like a good way for writers to publish their work? If so, why? If not, why not?

A writer may choose to only release her self-published work as an e-book or e-story. That way, she doesn't have to pay for printing a book that might not sell. Then websites like Amazon.com can sell the e-book to people around the world. There are even websites that help writers publish their works on their own.

THE MUSIC INDUSTRY

The music industry is a slightly different story than the publishing industry. Hopeful musicians who write their own lyrics will be dealing with the music business rather than publishers. However, there are a lot of similarities between the two.

A music label signs most popular musicians. There are currently three huge music companies: Universal, Sony, and Warner. However, there are also plenty of smaller companies that work with musical artists and writers too. And some musicians have created their own labels to distribute their music and then find new artists to release.

Text-Dependent Questions

1. Approximately what percentage of writers work for themselves?
2. According to the sidebar, what sorts of industries hire writers who don't work for themselves?
3. What is a publishing imprint?
4. Why might a writer choose to self-publish a book?
5. How many large music companies are there in the world currently? Are they the only options for artists who want to release music?

Music writers may also self-publish their work. They can produce CDs or MP3 files and release them directly to customers through their performances or websites. Even more ***established*** musicians sometimes self-publish, like Radiohead's 2007 release of *In Rainbows*. Musicians and music writers have a lot of choices these days.

Words to Understand

nonprofits: Companies that aren't trying to make money.
formal: Official or the regular way of doing things.
narration: A description of events in a story.

Chapter Four

How Do I Get Involved in Writing?

You may already be able to call yourself a writer. Do you write poems, stories, song lyrics, or raps for fun? If so, you're a writer! What's missing is being a professional writer, if that's what you want. Becoming a professional writer takes some hard work.

PRACTICE AND IMPROVE

If you want to be a professional writer, your first step is to practice. Once in a while, you'll hear about some amazing teen who published her first book and made millions, but that hardly ever happens. You're much better off putting in the time and hard work of writing practice than hoping for a stroke of good luck.

Write whenever you can. All sorts of writing counts, from essays

Taking writing classes or workshops in which you share your writing with other writers can help make you a better writer.

for school, to poems, to short stories, and beyond. The more you write, the more comfortable you'll be and the better you'll get.

You should also read a lot. Reading other people's language and stories is a good way to get a sense of what professional writing is like. You can find your own style and voice by reading other people's. Again, it doesn't really matter what you read, as long as you read a lot.

CLASSES

Some people are naturally better at writing than others, but writing is a learned art, and one that everyone can improve. Writing classes are a great way to learn writing tips, practice writing, and maybe start a major work.

As a middle or high school student, you'll of course be writing a lot. You'll write essays, lab reports, tests, and more. Use those writing times to really think about how to write well. That's partly what English class is for, after all! Writing in school helps you figure out how to come up with a thesis—a main idea—and also how to use correct grammar and how to structure writing so that it flows and is easy to read.

You may also be able to take creative writing classes, if that's what you're interested in. Some schools offer a class that focuses on writing creative works like fictional short stories, novels, and poems. If your school doesn't offer this kind of class, there may be an organization in your town or city that does. **Nonprofits** and community education centers often hold creative writing classes that are open to anyone.

Some writers focus on writing during college too. They major in creative writing, poetry, history of literature, or English. Then they get a lot of writing practice and guidance. Some people even go on to get a master's degree in these subjects.

However, professional authors often don't have *formal* training in writing. They just love to write, and have written their whole lives.

Almost every kind of writing will require research. Whether you're writing fiction or a news story for an Internet blog, you'll have to be sure you know about your subject.

Make Connections: Helpful Skills

You won't find a hard and fast list of skills you need to be a successful writer, but some skills are definitely helpful. If you've got these skills under your belt, you're on your way to becoming a professional writer. They include:

- good grammar and form
- imagination
- an eye for detail
- patience
- an open mind
- professionalism

They didn't necessarily major in writing in college, but they did work hard to improve their writing over time.

DO YOUR RESEARCH

Writing is more than just writing. Good writing is also all about research, even if it's fiction. If you're writing about a subject you don't know much about, you'll have to do some research to make sure you know what you're talking about. Even if you do know about your subject, you probably don't know everything there is to know about it, so you'll still have to do some research.

Let's say you're writing a short story about someone who travels around the world. If you're setting your story in the real world, you'll have to research each place your character travels to get an accurate

The most difficult part of writing is starting a piece or new project, especially when you work for yourself.

depiction of the region. You could make up something, but you probably won't get a good reception from publishers (or readers), and you won't look knowledgeable.

JUST WRITE!

You can do all the planning and practicing you want, but eventually it'll be time to write what you really want to write. If you feel ready to tackle your masterpiece, or even if you don't, start writing it! You'll never know how to do it until you try.

Mary Dodd, the author of *The Writer's Compass: From Story Map to Finished Draft in 7 Stages*, offers the following seven steps to help budding writers of short stories and novels.

1. Developing Ideas. Write down your ideas on index cards, sticky notes, or on a computer. Don't worry about the flow of the ideas, just write them all down.
2. Building a Strong Structure. Arrange your ideas into a story map, which is an outline of your story. Once you arrange all your ideas, you can see what's missing from your story and add them in.
3. Creating Vibrant Characters. Flesh out who is going to populate your story and make them into people with interesting personalities, behaviors, values, and ideas.
4. Structuring Scenes, Sequences, and Transitions. Once you have the overall flow of the story, create individual scenes. You also need to figure out how to transition from one scene to the next, to keep the story going.
5. Pacing and Tension. Add more details to your story, which contribute to the overall mood of each scene and the transitions between them. Make sure the story doesn't go too fast or too slowly for readers to enjoy it.
6. Enriching Language and Dialogue. After the storyline is filled in and the details fleshed out, you can focus on the details of the language you used. Choose appropriate words and style for the **narration** and each of your characters.

New techology—from the Internet to tablet computers—has changed the way writers can get their work read and make money with their art.

7. Editing and Submitting. The final step before sending it off is to read and reread your work, adjusting for content, grammar, and spelling. Then submit it to publishers, or publish it yourself!

Of course, some of these suggestions might not work for you. Everyone has a different writing process that is most helpful, and writing will help you figure out what yours is.

You might be able to find a writers' group to join, to help you write. Writers' groups are made up of individuals who want some support in their writing process. Some writers' groups may provide training and advice, while others simply offer a space for writers to come together and share their work. Writers' groups may be especially helpful if you find yourself stuck or suffering from writer's block. You'll also be able to meet contacts that can help you publish your work. Maybe one of your fellow writers knows a publisher who might be interested in exactly the kind of writing you're doing. Or maybe one of the writers is a publisher herself!

WRITE IN OTHER FIELDS

Publishing your artistic work of literature will probably take quite a while, between writing it and getting a publisher. In the meantime, write other things. Experiment with writing outside the published artistic field. Try journalism or copywriting. Writing articles for a newspaper, magazine, or website may not be exactly what you want to do, but it is writing. The more you can get your name out there as a writer, the better. Start with your school newspaper, or try to get a story into your local newspaper.

You can also try blogging for a while. You can post your own original work for others to read on a blog. A personal blog is a great way to test out your poems, short stories, and other work on a small audience. If you get positive receptions from regular readers and other writers, you can be more confident about what you're doing. Blogs are also a good space to get feedback on your work from a lot of

Becoming a successful writer can be difficult, but staying positive in the face of set-backs or rejections is key to making writing a career.

people, before you formally publish. Your blog may even catch the eye of a good contact that can help you get published.

REACH OUT TO PUBLISHERS

When you feel like your writing is ready to be published, then is the time to start reaching out to publishers. Do some research first. Publishers focus on different kinds of works, so you want to target your own manuscript to the publishers that match. If, for example, you've written a science fiction book, find the publishers that seem to already have a lot of science fiction books. That means they probably already have an editor or editors who work with science fiction writers, and know how to distribute and market science fiction books.

You also need to be ready to actually listen to publishers. They may send your manuscripts back and tell you things you don't want to hear. Some publishers might tell you that your piece is well written, but that very few readers would be interested in the subject matter you've written about. Other publishers may be interested, but need you to make significant changes before they'd be willing to publish your work. If you disagree with them and don't make any changes, you're staying true to your original writing, but you may have a lot of trouble getting it published. You should pick and choose which pieces of advice you listen to—publishers know a lot about what will sell, so if you're okay making the changes, go for it.

And you may get rejected from a lot of other publishers, or even never hear back from some of them. Don't give up! A lot of the most popular authors were rejected by publishers many times before they found one that was willing to take a chance.

If you've been trying for a long time, and you really think your work has the potential to attract a lot of attention, or if you just want to be a published author, think about self-publishing.

Research Project

This chapter gives you one version of the writing process, as outlined by Mary Dodd. Not every writer will follow this version, or find it helpful. Find another version of the writing process online and compare it to the one in this book. Which one appeals more to your way of writing? Do you think you would find any of the steps you find in either version helpful if you incorporated them into your own writing process?

MAKING IT BIG IN THE MUSIC INDUSTRY

Music writers can make it big in the music industry if they try hard and meet the right people. How you find success will depend on whether you also play music, or if you prefer just to write it. If you prefer to just write, you might find a musician who prefers just to perform and is looking for someone to write songs for her. If you write and play, you'll be on your own.

Musicians in the past mostly just tried to get signed by a record label. Today, that is only one of a few choices when it comes to being a successful musician. Instead of running after a label, you can also just release your music yourself and play as many shows as possible. As you get better and better, you can play at better venues and reach wider audiences. If you're lucky, audiences will really love your music, and spread the word. Before you know it, you could have a huge fan base and may even attract the attention of a record label (or have enough money to start your own).

Text-Dependent Questions

1. How can you use your time in school to get better at writing?
2. If you want formal training in writing, where might you look for classes?
3. How can blogging help you become a successful writer?
4. What kinds of publishers should you look for if you're ready to send them your writing?
5. What are your options when it comes to getting your music lyrics and music heard by an audience?

Of course, breaking into the music and publishing worlds can be tough. Not everyone will make it, but a mix of determination, skill, contacts, and luck just might get you there. You'll know that as a writer you're continuing on a tradition that stretches back thousands of years, whether you write raps, song lyrics, novels, or poems.

Find Out More

Online

Kid Pub
www.kidpub.com

Scribblitt Self-Publishing
www.scribblitt.com

Stone Soup
www.stonesoup.com

Time for Kids: Writing Tips
www.timeforkids.com/homework-helper/writing-tips

Writing Classes for Kids
writingclassesforkids.com/free-stuff/want-to-be-a-writer

In Books

Burke, Jim. *Writing Reminders: Tools, Tips, and Techniques*. Portsmouth, N.H.: Heinemann, 2003.

Donoghue, Carol. *The Story of Writing*. Buffalo, N.Y.: Firefly Books, 2007.

Fletcher, Ralph. *Poetry Matters: Writing a Poem from the Inside Out.* New York: HarperCollins, 2002.

Levine, Gail Carson. *Writing Magic: Creating Stories That Fly.* New York: HarperCollins, 2013.

Potter, Ellen and Anne Mazer. *Spilling Ink: A Young Writer's Handbook.* New York: Roaring Brook Press, 2010.

Series Glossary of Key Terms

Abstract: Made up of shapes that are symbolic. You might not be able to tell what a piece of abstract art is just by looking at it.

Classical: A certain kind of art traditional to the ancient Greek and Roman civilizations. In music, it refers to music in a European tradition that includes opera and symphony and that is generally considered more serious than other kinds of music.

Culture: All the arts, social meanings, thoughts, and behaviors that are common in a certain country or group.

Gallery: A room or a building that displays art.

Genre: A category of art, all with similar characteristics or styles.

Impressionism: A style of painting that focuses more on the artist's perception of movement and lighting than what something actually looks like.

Improvisation: Created without planning or preparation.

Medium (media): The materials or techniques used to create a work of art. Oil paints are a medium. So is digital photography.

Pitch: How high or low a musical note is; where it falls on a scale.

Portfolio: A collection of some of the art an artist has created, to show off her talents.

Realism: Art that tries to show something exactly as it appears in real life.

Renaissance: A period of rapid artistic and literary development during the 1500s–1700s, or the name of the artistic style from this period.

Studio: A place where an artist can work and create his art.

Style: A certain way of creating art specific to a person or time period.

Technique: A certain way of creating a piece of art.

Tempo: How fast a piece of music goes.

Venue: The location or facility where an event takes place.

ST. JOHN THE BAPTIST PARISH LIBRARY
2920 NEW HIGHWAY 51
LAPLACE, LOUISIANA 70068

Index

About the Author

Sara James is a writer and blogger. She writes educational books for children on a variety of topics, including health, history, and current events.

Picture Credits

6: Rido | Dreamstime.com
12: Blue Marble
14: Brian Stansberry
16: U.S. National Archives
18: Scholastic Books
20: 350jb | Dreamstime.com
22: Marie-Lan Nguyen
23: Kvitoshka | Dreamstime.com
24: Pline
26: Marcus Cyron
30: Angie Schwendemann
32: Maurilbert
34: Krutov Igor | Dreamstime.com
36: Syda Productions - Fotolia.com
37: Josie - Fotolia.com
38: Orlando Bellini - Fotolia.com
40: Raluca Tudor | Dreamstime.com
44: Natee Srisuk | Dreamstime.com
46: Igor Mojzes - Fotolia.com
48: Koufax73 - Fotolia.com
50: Aron Hsiao - Fotolia.com
52: manaemedia - Fotolia.com
54: Arenacreative | Dreamstime.com